Linux Network Administration Pocketbook

Zico Pratama Putra

Kanzul Ilmi Press

2018

First Printing: 2018

ISBN-13: 978-1722096960

ISBN-10: 1722096969

Kanzul Ilmi Press

High Street.

London, UK

Bookstores and wholesalers: Please contact Kanzul Ilmi Press email

zico.pratama@gmail.com.

Trademark Acknowledgments

Ordering Information: Special discounts are available on quantity purchases by corporations, associations, educators, and others. For details, contact the publisher at the above-listed address.

contents

Linux Network Administrator / Network Configuration

Installation of the network adapter

Network cards are often detected at startup. If this is not the case it will load the corresponding modules.

For a list of network interfaces that have been detected, you can use the command

ifconfig

The sections that start with ethX match the cards ethernet where X is the number of the card. If

the card is not detected, it will load the module with the command

modprobe <module name>

Some common modules can be noted: ne2k-pci for NE2000 cards, via-rhine, rtl8139 ...

The modules available for your kernel are located in / lib / modules / <kernel name> / kernel / drivers / net /.

The following command displays the network modules available for the kernel in use:

ls / lib / modules / `uname -r` / kernel / drivers / net /

For the name of the function module of the trade name of a card, a search on the internet is often the best solution.

The core may provide useful information about network cards. Posts containing one can search "eth0" for more information on the first detected network card:

dmesg | grep eth0

The following command displays the network cards connected to the bus PCI :

lspci | grep Ethernet

Configuring the Network Interface

Once your card recognized by the kernel, you must at least specify the IP address and subnet mask of subnet map. In the case of a local network connected to the Internet, you must also add the IP address of the gateway and IP address of one or more DNS servers.

IP adress

To assign an IP address to a network interface, you can use the ifconfig command:

ifconfig <interface> <ip address>

For example :

ifconfig eth0 192.168.1.12

The subnet mask is automatically determined according to the class address IP. If it is different you can specify it with the netmask option:

ifconfig eth0 192.168.1.12 netmask 255.255.255.128

To see if the network card is configured, you can use the command:

ifconfig eth0

Gateway and Routing

To add a gateway, you can use the route command:

route add default gw <IP address>

To view the routes to different networks:

route -n

Test the network

To test whether the network card is working, we can try to communicate with another machine with the command

ping <ip address>

The ping command sends a packet to the IP address and then waits for the machine responds. It then displays the time it took the entire operation, in milliseconds.

Information interfaces

To check the status of all the interfaces you can use the command

netstat -a

Host Name (hostname)

The / etc / hostname contains the name of the machine. Just edit it to change the host name of the machine. This change is not immediately taken into account by the system. It will be the next time the machine or after launching:

/etc/init.d/hostname.sh

It can also change the host name with the following command, but it will not be kept on the next boot:

hostname <hostname>

Automatic configuration at boot

The / etc / network / interfaces to configure permanently NICs.

For example :

auto lo
iface lo inet loopback

auto eth0
iface eth0 inet static
    address 192.168.1.2
    netmask 255.255.255.0
    gateway 192.168.1.1

This configuration automatically initialize interfaces "lo" and "eth0".

The "lo" interface is often essential to the system, it is important to initialize. It will systematically the IP address 127.0.0.1.

The "eth0" interface will be configured with the IP address 192.168.1.2, subnet mask 192.168.1.1 255.255.255.0 and the gateway (this is optional).

If eth0 to be configured automatically by a server DHCP, you must specify:

auto eth0
iface eth0 inet dhcp

For changes to this file to take effect, restart or use the ifup and ifdown commands. For example :

ifup eth0

Host Name Resolution

The /etc/host.conf file specifies how names should be resolved (ie how to move from an IP address to a name, and vice versa). For example :

First translate with DNS servers and then with / etc / hosts. order bind, hosts

There are machines with multiple addresses
multi on

Verifies IP spoofing is nospoof

DNS servers

/etc/resolv.conf contains the IP addresses of servers DNS. For example :

nameserver 208.164.186.1
nameserver 208.164.186.2
search foo

The search command indicates that if a domain name is not found, it will try by adding .foo.

hosts file

The / etc / hosts file contains a list of name resolution (IP addresses and machine names). For example:

192.168.105.2 sasa

This file indicates that sasa is the IP address 192.168.105.2, which will be accessible by this alias.

Network administration Linux / NFS

The protocol NFS (Network file system) allows you to share files between machines Unix, and so Linux.It is a client-server model: a machine provides (exports) directories from its local file system on the network. Next the access rights, the other network stations can mount these directories, which will then be seen as local directories. A computer can be both client and NFS server.

server-side installation

Start by checking that the NFS daemons (nfsd) are already underway with, for example, the command

ps ax | grep nfsd

To start the daemons manually under Debian:

/etc/init.d/nfs-kernel-server start

or, if the NFS server userspace that is installed:

/etc/init.d/nfs-user-server start

We can start by replacing restart to restart the server.

Configuration

To share (or export) directories, you must inform the / etc / exports. It shows the list of shared folders and names of machines that can access it.
Each line corresponds to a directory and has the form:

<Local directory> <name or IP of the machines allowed to connect> (<options>) <other machines> (<options>) ...

For example :

/ Home / bobollinux (rw) station 1 (ro)
/project   station1 (rw) (ro)
/draft copy

The server exports the / home directory. The ollinux machine can mount it read / write (rw), read-only station 1 (ro), and the other machines will not connect.
Similarly, station 1 may access read / write to the project directory and all other stations read only.
Finally, everyone can access read / write to the draft folder (the rw option is the default).
To know the list of possible options and their meanings, see man exports.

Note that write access via the network will still inhibited by the rights to the file system. Consider a test file owned by root, located in the project directory and with the rights 600 (read / write for root only, no rights for others). If foo user accesses via the station 1 station directory / project, it can not access the test file, although it has the "rights network read-write".
Once the file / etc / exports properly configured, simply restart the NFS service with the following command for the changes to take effect:

/etc/init.d/nfs-kernel-server reload

client side installation

This is relatively simple since the NFS "network file system" is directly built into the kernel. Just check that it has been compiled with support for NFS. This is true of all recent distributions.

To mount a remote file system, use the mount command with the nfs option:

mount -t nfs <remote machine>: <shared directory> <local directory> -o <options>

For example :

mount -t nfs 192.168.105.2:/armor/plages / mnt / o ro ratings

This command will mount the / armor / tracks, exported by 192.168.105.2 station in the local directory / mnt / ratings, read-only.

Instead of an IP address, you can also give a host name, such sasa. For this, we need the name sasa can be converted to IP address (by modifying / etc / hosts for example, if you have no DNS server)

Login to start

It is possible to connect the shared directories on startup of the station.

The easiest way is to fill the / etc / fstab file that contains a list of known file systems.

The syntax is:

<Remote computer>: <remote directory> <local directory> nfs <options> 0 0

In the previous example, it would:

sasa: / armor / tracks / mnt / nfs car odds, rw, user, soft 0 0

The options are described in the mount man page. Some are common to other file systems (ext2, vfat ...) while others are specific to NFS.

Network administration Linux / Samba

Samba is a service for sharing folders and printers between Linux workstations and Windows workstations. A comprehensive How-To can be found there:http: / / www. samba. org / samba / docs /man / Samba-HOWTO-Collection /

This section presents just an introduction to the use of Samba. We consider that we use safe mode (security = user requires a user account unix). Use the domain security level and the game part sharing with Windows (including the latest version) is not seen. To access a Windows This page gives some additional commands:http://www.oregontechsupport.com/samba/samba.php

Samba Service Configuration

To configure this service to change the main file is smb.conf usually located in / etc or / etc / samba as distribution.

There are also graphical interfaces to configure Samba.

The [global] section contains options common to all shared directories.

Here are some useful options:

workgroup

> The name of the workgroup. The computers in the same workgroup can be found side by side in the Windows Network Neighborhood.

server string

> The description of the server, which will appear next to its name in Windows Explorer. If the description contains the word% h will be replaced by the host name of the machine.

encrypt passwords

> Determines whether passwords must be encrypted before being transmitted. It is highly recommended and all Windows systems from 98 and NT4 SP3 use this feature by default.

log file

> The name of the file containing the activity log of the server. One can have a log per client machine using% m in the file name. The% m will be replaced with the name of the client machine.

max log size

> Maximum size of the log file, Kio.

socket options

> Indicates the options to put on *sockets* such TCP_NODELAY for the system to send small packets immediately without waiting to be several.

Many other options are available. They are detailed in the man page of smb.conf[1]

Example

[global]
workgroup = home
server string = Samba Server% h
encrypt passwords = true
log file = /var/log/samba/log.%m
max log size = 1000

socket options = TCP_NODELAY

Directories Sharing Setup

Samba shares are described in sections of the following form:

[<Share name>]
<Option> = <value>
...

The main parameters are:

how

> The description of the shared directory.

path

> The path to the shared directory. It is the content of this folder will be shared.

read only

> Determines whether guests can write or not in the shared directory.

public

> Whether to allow connections without password.

valid users

> List of authorized users to connect separated by spaces. If we want to allow all users do not set this option.

browseable

> Determines if the shares appear in the list of shares from the server.

The [homes] is a special sharing. It defines the sharing of user directories unix machine accounts.

Many other options are available. They are detailed in the man page of smb.conf[1]
Default (3.5.6 release) you can access anonymously samba (smbclient // server / sharename -U account without a password). For a more secure access (with account and password), you must also add a Samba account that reference to an existing Linux account: adduser account (if not done) smbpasswd account rights directories and files must be correct. Example chmod u + rws, g + rx, where rx + ... / folder and / or file

Examples

[CD-ROM]
comment = Samba server's CD-ROM
read only = yes
locking = no
path = / cdrom
guest ok = yes

[sharing]
path = / media / d / Share
available = yes
browsable = yes
public = yes

writable = yes

[Zelinux]
comment = Website
path = / myrep / zelinux
read only = no

Protect shared directories

You can make a private directory and whether to allow users to access them.

For this, for each shared folder add the options:

public = no
valid users = <name of authorized users to access directories>

For each name you've entered, add the user with samba

smbpasswd -a <username>

A unix account of the same name must exist. If it does not, create it with adduser.

Service launch

launch:

/etc/init.d/samba start

To stop:

/etc/init.d/samba stop

To restart:

/etc/init.d/samba restart

Changes in smb.conf are taken into account for each new connection. To make them effective on already established connections must restart Samba.

Directory Access

To access the share in Windows, simply open the neighborhood networks a Windows station and check if the machine is there.
To connect from the command line to a share from Linux, you can use the command

smbclient // <server name> / <share name> -U <user>

It is also possible to mount a Samba share with

smbmount // <server name> / <share name> <local directory>

Different options are available. Can be found in the man   smbclient   and man smbmount.
Generally, it is advisable to add -o username = account, password = ??? to log in.

For example, to mount a "public" directory must specify the need to connect as a guest:

smbmount // server / share / mountpoint -o guest

It also requires that your user account has the rights to assembly. The root account can use smbmount without much problem.

Otherwise, there are several possibilities:

1. complete the file / etc / fstab with your mounting // <IP ADDRESS> / <folder_on share>
   <your_local_mountpoint cifs defaults, iocharset = utf8, codepage = cp850, uid = 1000, gid = 1000, noauto, user, credentials = ~ /.smb 0 0)

2. add rights in sudoers. (By default in Ubuntu 10.10, sudo smbclient // <name server> / <share name> <local directory> -o username = account, password = ??? works well)

References

[1] http://us1.samba.org/samba/docs/man/manpages-3/smb.conf.5.html

Network administration Linux / Apache

Apache is a server HTTP free. An HTTP server lets you host Web sites to be accessed with a Navigator such as Mozilla Firefox, Internet Explorer or Chromium.

A website can provide any type of content (text files, HTML, Flash, zip...). This content can be static (the server sends a file to the browser) or dynamic (the content is generated by a program executed by the server). The websites usually contain several types of documents, some are static and other dynamic.

We deal here with Apache 2.2 on a system Debian (And its derivatives, such as Ubuntu).

log files

Debian default, Apache logs errors in the /var/log/apache2/error.log file. When something does not work, this file often provides clues to find the solution.

It also records all requests in /var/log/apache2/access.log.

Basic Configuration

On Debian, Apache launches automatically when installs and every system startup. When changing the configuration, you must make him aware of the changes with the command

/etc/init.d/apache2 reload

To stop, start or restart the we use the same command with stop, start or restart.

[1]

Server Configuration

The configuration [2]the server is in /etc/apache2/apache2.conf. This file contains include statements[3]which are used to move parts of the configuration in other files. Debian uses this feature for modules[4] (Like PHP) and management of virtual servers [5] :

Configuring Modules

The / etc / apache2 / mods-available contains the modules installed. The / etc / apache2 / mods-enabled contains modules enabled. The activated modules aresymlinks to the installed modules.

To enable or disable a module, you can directly manipulate the links or use the a2enmod a2dismod and controls (see the man pages).

Configuring Sites

Similarly, the / etc / apache2 / sites-available contains the available websites and / etc / apache2 / sites-enabled enabled sites. There are pre-installed: the default website.

Sites can be activated or deactivated by manipulating the links in sites-enabled or using a2ensite and a2dissite.

Some basic guidelines

The syntax of Apache's pretty simple. There are blocks (or contexts) such as:

<VirtualHost ...> # start VirtualHost block

...

   <Directory ...> Directory block beginning #

    ...

   </ Directory>   # End of block Directory

...

</ VirtualHost>   # End of VirtualHost block

and guidelines such as

Include / etc / apache2 / sites-enabled /

The guidelines for configuring the server itself are generally placed in apache2.conf. Those that concern only website are offset in the site configuration file (sites-available / my-website-web).

The directive DocumentRoot [6]Fixed the web server root, that is to say the base directory where the documents are. For example with the directive DocumentRoot / var / www / html, if the browser requests the page http: //serveur/repertoire/fichier.txt, the server will look /var/www/html/repertoire/fichier.txt the file.

UserDir [7]to specify the home directory of the system users. The directive UserDir public_html means a user can publish their personal web pages in a public_html subdirectory of your home directory. For the user toto, it is usually / home / foo / public_html. Its home page will be accessible through the special URL http: // server / ~ toto.

DirectoryIndex [8]shows the list of files that Apache will look to see if the URL does not specify. For example if the configuration contains DirectoryIndex index.html index.php and ask the URL http: // server / directory /, Apache will look in the directory an index.html or index.php. If any of these files exist, it will be displayed. Otherwise, Apache will either display the list of files, an error (depending on the presence of Indexes in the Options directive[9]).

AccessFileName [10]defines the name of the file that can be placed in a directory to modify its configuration. This allows, for example, prohibit locally displaying the file list, or password protect a directory and its subdirectories.

listen [11] tells Apache on which Harbor TCP he must listen. HTTP protocol The default port is 80.

ServerName[12]tells Apache its domain name and possibly its port. He uses it when it needs to communicate his address to the client (browser). This is the case for example when requesting http: // server / directory without slash (/) at the end. As this is not a valid URL (the URL of a directory must end with a slash), Apache uses the ServerName to rebuild an address with a slash and the reference to the customer.

Management of the number of instances of Apache

The Apache server uses several processes and take care of several types of multi-processor stations using MPMs (Multi processing modules).

The first module uses prefork processes (for stable or older systems), the second worker uses threads, and the last of threads per process. Last perchild module is under development and is not recommended.

The one used by default in Linux is prefork.

commented example

The part of the configuration file management processing in the number of processes and the following:

```
##
## Server-Pool Size Regulation (MPM specific) ##

# prefork MPM
# StartServers ......... nb server processes at startup
# MinSpareServers nb ...... minimum of process servers " 'free' "
  instantiateds
# MaxSpareServers nb ...... maximum process servers " 'free' "
  instantiated. S 'he there are MaxSpareServers + 1 we kill them
# MaxClients ........... up servers that can process nb start

# Nb .. MaxRequestsPerChild maximum of requests handled by the server process.

#                              After MaxRequestsPerChild requests, the
process dies.
#                              If MaxRequestsPerChild = 0, then the process
not'expired never.

<IfModule prefork.c>
  StartServers 5
  MinSpareServers 5
  MaxSpareServers 10
```

```
    MaxClients 20
    MaxRequestsPerChild 0
</ IfModule>
```

pthread MPM # StartServers .... *initial number of server* processes **to start**

MaxClients .... *maximum number of server processes allowed to* start

MinSpareThreads ...... **minimum number of worker threads are qui** kept **spare**

MaxSpareThreads ...... *maximum number of worker threads are qui* kept **spare**

ThreadsPerChild ...... *constant number of worker threads in Each* server **process**

MaxRequestsPerChild .. *maximum number of requests a server process* reserves

```
<IfModule worker.c>
    StartServers 2
    MaxClients 150
    MinSpareThreads 25
    MaxSpareThreads 75
    ThreadsPerChild 25
    MaxRequestsPerChild 0
</ IfModule>
```

perchild MPM # NUMSERVERS .... *constant number of server* processes

StartThreads .... **initial number of worker threads in Each** server **process**

MinSpareThreads ...... *minimum number of worker threads are qui* kept **spare**

MaxSpareThreads ...... *maximum number of worker threads are qui* kept **spare**

MaxThreadsPerChild ... *maximum number of worker threads in Each* server **process**

MaxRequestsPerChild .. *Maximum number of connections per server* process **(Then it dies)**

```
<IfModule perchild.c>
    NUMSERVERS 5
    StartThreads 5
    MinSpareThreads 5
    MaxSpareThreads 10
    MaxThreadsPerChild 20
    MaxRequestsPerChild 0
    AcceptMutex fcntl
```

</ IfModule>

Setting directories

Each directory to which Apache accesses can be configured independently (and its subdirectories inherit).

Setting a directory is placed in a "container" delimited by <Directory chemin_du_répertoire> and </ Directory>. The configuration applies to the directory and all subdirectories. If a subdirectory also has its own configuration, it is added to the parent.

Here are some examples of access control. More details are given in "A sample configuration."

Configuring the system root directory <Directory />

    # It does not authorize any particular option None
    Options

    # No changes are allowed in .htaccess files AllowOverride None

</ Directory>

For the server root: <Directory / var
/ www / html>
    # some options
    Options Indexes Includes FollowSymLinks

    # The options can be changed in a .htaccess AllowOverride All

    # Allows everyone to access Allow from All Documents

    # Specifies how to apply the previous rule Order allow, deny
</ Directory>

The directory containing executable CGI <Directory / usr /
lib / cgi-bin>
    AllowOverride None
    Options ExecCGI
</ Directory>

The possible parameters of the Options directive [13] are: "None", "All", "Indexes", "Includes", "FollowSymLinks", "ExecCGI" or "MultiViews".

Manage personal webpages

It is possible that users of the system to broadcast personal pages without having to create a user site. This requires the use userdir module.

The directory containing the website should be created in the home of the user and should be readable for all. The directory name is defined by the directive UserDir[7]. By default this is the public_html directory.

The address to access these personal sites is the user name preceded by a tilde (~).

For example, a user foo on www.iut.clermont.fr server can create the pages of its site in the / home / foo / public_html, and we can access them with the http: //www.iut. clermont.fr/~toto/.

You can allow only certain users to benefit from UserDir. For example, to allow only sasa toto and to have a personal website:

UserDir disabled
UserDir enabled sasa toto

To set options for these directories, you can use a clause to the Directory / home / * / public_html:

<Directory / home / * / public_html>
    Order allow, deny
    Allow from all
</ Directory>

The UserDir public_html clause only works for users with an account on the system. The URLhttp: / / www. IUT. Clermont. en / foo ~only works if foo is a real user (in which case the term Unix ~ toto makes sense), not only if the directory / home / foo / public_html exists

another form of UserDir can be used to allow the directories without necessarily there is a unix account associated:

UserDir / home / * / public_html

CGI scripts

Write a CGI program

The CGI (Common Gateway Interface) is not a language, it is a standard. A CGI program can be written in any language (C, Java, PHP, bash ...), provided that it is executable and it complies with certain input / output constraints.

The main constraint is the exit. If a CGI program generates data to its standard output, it must precede an http header to identify them. Here is an example CGI program written in bash:

```
#! / Bin / bash

# Header
echo "Content-type: text / html"

#  Late header echo ""
```

Content to display in the browser echo "<html>
<body> Hello </ body> </ html>"

This script generates an HTML page.

Configure access to CGI scripts

For Apache supports scripting, it is necessary to perform a minimum of setup in the site configuration.
The statement ScriptAlias / cgi-bin path specifies the name of the authorized directory containing scripts
CGI. example:

ScriptAlias / cgi-bin / var / www / cgi-bin

The path / cgi-bin does not really exist, it is directed to / var / www / cgi-bin, and it allows you to write URL
like http: // server / cgi-bin / myscript.
The active following clause the ExecCGI option in / var / www / cgi-bin, allowing Apache to execute scripts
on the server:

<Directory / var / www / cgi-bin>
   ExecCGI options
</ Directory>

Example: you write a script essai.cgi, and you want / home / httpd / cgi-bin contains the scripts. Therefore
at least write:

ScriptAlias / cgi-bin / home / httpd / cgi-bin
<Directory / var / www / cgi-bin>
   ExecCGI options
</ Directory>

The call for a script essai.cgi will be made by the URL: http: //serveur/cgi-bin/essai.cgi

The PHP module

PHP has normally been integrated into the Apache server as a loadable module located like other Apache
modules in / usr / lib / apache2 / modules.
The /etc/apache2/mods-availiable/php.load and /etc/apache2/mods-availiable/php.conf files contain
LoadModule and AddType directives that allow Apache to run PHP when requesting a file ending in .php.
They must be linked to / etc / apache2 / mods-enabled to enable PHP. One can use it to control the
a2enmod.
On the sidelines of Apache, PHP has also its configuration file, often /etc/php.ini. It is particularly advisable
to intervene unless you know what you're doing. that we can nevertheless observe PHP takes into
consideration the MySQL plugin, containing access functions "engine" of MySQL database (which had to
be installed separately), by the presence of extension = mysql .so.
When changing a configuration file as PHP runs as an Apache module, restart Apache to PHP reset by
reading php.ini.

/etc/init.d/apache2 restart

Password protection

There are a lot of solutions to protect password per site.

Apache provides a simple solution to protect a directory and its subdirectories.

This requires using the .htaccess file and maintain a password file.

Authentication Configuration

The file .htaccess is located in the directory where it applies the rules.

in this file we will place the definition of restrictions.

It is imperative that the change of authentication parameters is allowed in the Apache

configuration.[14]

The guidelines in place in the .htaccess are:

AuthType basic

authentication type commonly adopted but insecure

AuthName "My message"

display the text as prompts in the dialog box

AuthUserFile / etc / apache2 / my_passwd

indicates where will the passwords

Require valid-user

states need an account in the password file to access the directory

You can also use Require user toto sasa to allow only toto accounts and sasa.

The authentication type basic circulated passwords in the clear. There are other types as more secure digest, it is recommended to combine../HTTPS/. See Article on Wikipedia for details on the operation.

The first request to this protected directory will bring up a dialog box through which the user must identify themselves (name and password):

• If the entered password is invalid, the dialog box will be displayed again.
• If valid, the browser saves and will not prompt more.

It will restart the browser to request it again.

password file

To maintain the password file we use the htpasswd command (see man page).

For example, to create the password file password / etc / apache2 / default-passwd with 1 as user foo, use the command

htpasswd -c / etc / apache2 / foo my_passwd

To add or edit a user to an existing password file:

htpasswd / etc / apache2 / my_passwd sasa

virtual server (virtual hosts)

Apache can handle multiple websites simultaneously. They will all be accessible from the same IP address and the same port.

To differentiate, Apache uses the address requested by the browser.

For example if site1.com site2.com and point to the same IP address, URL and http://site1.com/ http://site2.com/ lead on the same server.

But at the time of the request, the browser says he has asked the address http://site1.com/ or http://site2.com/.

Apache uses this information to know which site to view. We are talking about *Virtual server* or virtual host.

To tell Apache which site matches a domain name, a section using <VirtualHost *>. On Debian, it is usually a VirtualHost per file in the / etc / apache2 / sites-available.

The section should contain a ServerName [12] which will indicate the name associated with this virtual server. It may also contain a ServerAlias [15] if we want other names end in site.

For example :

<VirtualHost *>
   ServerAdmin admin@site1.com
   DocumentRoot / home / site1 / root
   ServerName site1.com
   ServerAlias www.site1.com
   AccessLog /home/site1/access.log
   ErrorLog /home/site1/error.log
   <Directory / home / site1 / root>
     AllowOverride All
   </ Directory>
</ VirtualHost>

The Apache documentation on virtual servers [5] contains detailed information on the subject.

For this virtual server is running, it is imperative that site1.com www.site1.com names and are known by the machine tries to access (the one that starts the browser).

For this there are several methods:

- buy the domain name in question and set it to point to the correct IP address
- use a DNS server that will return the correct IP for that domain
- modify the hosts file on the client machine to match the field with the correct IP address (see the book

   Installation and configuration of a network adapter)

Configuration examples

Examples of configuration. The set of possible directions can be found here:http: // httpd. apache.org/docs/2.2/mod/directives.html

Think that the guidelines may have to be in apache2.conf, sometimes in the context of a given site VirtualHost.

ServerType

ServerType standalone

This line indicates if the Apache server starts in autonomous (standalone) or via inetd (tcp_wrapper). For most configuration, standalone. This directive has disappeared from Apache 2, which has another way to define it. The behavior is actually selected after the MTM (Multi-processing module) selected.

ServerRoot

ServerRoot / etc / apache2

(Config server only, not in a VirtualHost)

Here you specify the Apache installation directory. Normally the installation scripts were well informed that line. Check it anyway.

LockFile

LockFile /var/run/httpd.lock

(Config server only, not in a VirtualHost)

Leave this line as it is, ie commented in 90% of cases (to #).

PidFile

PidFile /var/run/httpd.pid

(Config server only, not in a VirtualHost)

Make sure that this line is uncommented. It tells the startup script to register the Apache process number for when stopping the Apache process system is stopped correctly.

ScoreBoardFile

ScoreBoardFile /var/run/httpd.scoreboard

(Config server only, not in a VirtualHost)

This file stores information for the functioning of Apache.

timeout

timeout 300

(Config server only, not in a VirtualHost)

Time in seconds before the server sends or receives a timeout. When the server is waiting for a "response" (eg, CGI, connection \ ldots), if after that time he receives no response, it will stop and prevent the user of the error. Leave this default unless you are working properly, particularly treatments that exceed this limit. Do not go too high either because this value if the external program "planted" or if an error occurred, you may make it inaccessible Apache for too long (it is always unpleasant to wait for anything).

KeepAlive

KeepAlive is

Whether to allow persistent connections (multiple queries by connections). In fact it allows users to your server to run multiple applications at once, and thus accelerate server responses. Let this default most of the time. For small servers leave this option on it. For a busy server, as soon as you notice that the system slows dramatically or become unavailable often try to off. But first, try lowering the value to the next option.

MaxKeepAliveRequests

MaxKeepAliveRequests 100

In combination with the previous option, shows the number of requests for a connection. Let this pretty high value for very good performance. If you set 0 as the value, you actually allow unlimited (so be careful). Leave the default value too.

KeepAliveTimeout

KeepAliveTimeout 15

waiting value in seconds before the next request from the same client on the same connection, before returning a timeout. Again leave the default.

MinSpareServers & MaxSpareServer

MinSpareServers 5
MaxSpareServer 10

(Config server only, not in a VirtualHost)

These values are used to self-regulating server load. In fact Apache itself controls its load, depending on the number of customers it serves and the number of requests that each customer demand. He made sure that everyone can be served alone and adds a number of instances Apaches "idle", that is to say that do nothing but are ready to serve new clients that would connect. If this number is less than MinSpareServers it adds one (or more). If this number exceeds the value of MaxSpareServer it stops in one (or more). These defaults are suitable for most sites.

listen

listen 3000
listen 12.34.56.78
listen 12.34.56.78:3000

Tell server ports or IP addresses (there is a network interface by the server!), Or both, where it needs to "listen" connection requests, IN ADDITION address and default port. See Directive VirtualHost further.

BindAdress

BindAdress *

Redundant with Listen, this allows you to specify IP addresses of network interfaces to listen for requests. This directive has disappeared in Apache 2.

Harbor

Port 80

Listen with redundant, it specifies the listening port (default 80). This directive has disappeared in Apache 2.

LoadModule, ClearModuleList & AddModule

LoadModule xxxxxx.mod libexec / yyyyyy.so
ClearModuleList
AddModule zzzz.c

(Config server only, not in a VirtualHost)
Support for DSO modules (Dynamic Shared Object). LoadModule is used to load a module. Before Apache 2, the ClearModuleList and AddModule directives allow you to specify the execution order of the modules because of dependency problems. Apache 2 can now do this automatically because the modules of APIs allows them to specify their own order. Apache 1. * must however be paying attention, and keep it current with the addition of any new module.

ExtendedStatus

ExtendedStatus it

(Config server only, not in a VirtualHost)
Specifies whether the server should return complete status information (on) or reduced information (off). off by default. Leave this default unless development and debugging.

User & Group

user nobody
Group nobody

After starting the server, it would be dangerous to leave it as root to answer queries. It is therefore possible to change the utiliseur and group process to give a minimum of rights on the server machine. (In fact, if someone comes to "exploit" your server, for example if you happen to execute code with the Apache server, it inherits the rights of the server itself. So if nobody does it no specific law. If it is a real or root user, then it will have the rights to damage your system.)

ServerAdmin

ServerAdmin root@localhost.domainname

E-mail address of the site administrator. This address is displayed by the server, for example in case of error, so that users can notify the administrator.

ServerName

ServerName www.domainname

Address that the server will return to the web client. It is best to put a resolved address by DNS instead of the name of the actual machine, so that visitors do not see the actual name of your machine (useful for safety too).

DocumentRoot

DocumentRoot / var / lib / apache / htdocs

root or is your web pages directory.

Directory

<Directory / var / lib / apache / htdocs>
    Options Indexes FollowSymlinks Multiviews
    AllowOverride None
    Order allow, deny
    Allow from all
</ Directory>

Change the settings of the directory / var / lib / apache / htdocs. Can be placed within the following guidelines:

options

the options are defined for this directory. The options are:

None	Disable all options.
All	Active all Multiviews EXCEPT options.
indexes	Allows users to have indexes generated by the server. That is, if the directory index (the index.html + often) is missing, it allows the server to list the directory contents (hazardous according to the content files in this directory).
FollowSymLinks	Allowed to follow symbolic links.
ExecCGI	Allow to run CGI scripts from this directory.
includes	Allows include files to the server.
IncludesNOEXEC	Enables but includes but prevents EXEC command (which allows to execute code).
MultiViews	Allows multiple views in a context. For example to display pages in a language according to the customer's language configuration.
SymLinksIfOwnerMatch	Allowed to follow links only if the user ID file (or directory) to which the link is the same as link.

AllowOverride

defines how managed .htaccess file in that directory:

All	Manages everything in .htaccess
AuthConfig	Enables AuthDBMGroupFile permissions guidelines AuthDBMUserFile, AuthGroupFile, AuthName, AuthType, AuthUserFile, Require etc.
FileInfo	Active features controlling the type of document (ErrorDocument, LanguagePriority, etc.)
Limit	Enable Limit Authorization Directive
None	Do not read the .htaccess file and let the "Linux" rights to that directory.
options	Active Directive Option

Order

Give the order of application of Allow / Deny:

deny, allow	If the client does not match any rule deny, but matches a rule allow, then we allow (allow by default).
allow, deny	If the client does not match any rules allow, but matches a rule deny, is prohibited (deny by default). \ Hline

Allow / Deny

Host Name	Allow / Deny the specified hosts, IP addresses, domain name, etc ...
All	Allow / Deny everyone

To you place your rules depending on the contents of your directory accessible by the web. There are the same rules for file (<Files> </ Files>) and rentals (<Location> </ Location>). See example for files (file) below.

DirectoryIndex

DirectoryIndex index.html index.htm index.php index.php5

Specifies the file to load when accessing a directory without specifying file. In this example, if you accesshttp://example.com/repertoire/, Apache will look for the listed files (index.html, index.htm ...) and if it finds one it will display. If it does not find one, it will display a list of files or deny access (depending on the presence or not of the Indexes option in the directory).

AccessFileName

.htaccess AccessFileName

File name of the access rules for AllowOverride rules. Tip: Place as seen above rule a line like:

```
<Files .ht *>          # to prohibit visitors to view the content of Order allow, deny
                       #fichiers .ht containing rules
    Deny from all # safety.
</ Files>
```

CacheNegotiatedDocs

#CacheNegotiatedDocs

Whether to allow proxies to cache documents (to allow, remove the comment # beginning of the line)

UseCanonicalName

It UseCanonicalName

Atop it, rewrites the URL to the values Server and port specified earlier in the httpd.conf.

On off, the URL remains the one given by the customer.

Attention is put on if you use CGI with SERVER_NAME variables because if the client's URL is not the same as CGI, your CGI script will not work.

DefaultType

DefaultType text / plain

mime type by default the server returns to clients. Fits in most cases.

HostNameLookups

HostNameLookups off

On one, client server name through reverse DNS query. Otherwise, he just IP address, which generates much less network traffic.

ErrorLog

ErrorLog / var / log / error_log

full file path where errors will be recorded.

LogLevel

LogLevel warn

Error recording level as possible with values, in descending order of importance, thus increasing chatter in:

emerg	Emergency: The server becomes unusable
alert	intervention is necessary
crit	critical errors (network access not for example)
error	errors in pages, scripts
warn	non-fatal errors (badly coded pages, scripts with non blocantes errors ...
notice	normal event but deserving to be noticed
info	information (such as "busy server")
debug	Saves ANYTHING can happen on the server

The criterion level is the recommended minimum, and generally amounts to warn.

ServerSignature

ServerSignature it

we	adds signature (Version, OS ...) when the server generates pages itself (missing index, script error, etc.)
off	only shows the error.
Mail adds a link to the email defined by ServerAdmin	

Alias

Alias faux_nom realname

allows for aliases directories (links somehow) (similar to ScriptAlias / cgi-bin chemin_complet_des_cgi

AddType

AddType kind extensions

(Under Apache 2, this Directive should be in a mod-file availabe / nom_module.conf instead of apache2.conf)

Specifies that files using such extensions are of the type specified. This will decide what to do. To add PHP support, the mods-enabled file / php5.conf contains for example:

```
AddType application / x-httpd-php .php .phtml .php3 AddType
application / x-httpd-php-source .phps
```

AddHandler

AddHandler cgi-script .cgi

To use CGI scripts.

References

[1] http://httpd.apache.org/docs/2.2/invoking.html
[2] http://httpd.apache.org/docs/2.2/configuring.html
[3] http://httpd.apache.org/docs/2.2/mod/core.html#include
[4] http://httpd.apache.org/docs/2.2/dso.html
[5] http://httpd.apache.org/docs/2.2/vhosts/
[6] http://httpd.apache.org/docs/2.2/mod/core.html#documentroot
[7] http://httpd.apache.org/docs/2.2/mod/mod_userdir.html#userdir
[8] http://httpd.apache.org/docs/2.2/mod/mod_dir.html#directoryindex
[9] http://httpd.apache.org/docs/1.3/mod/core.html#options
[10] http://httpd.apache.org/docs/2.2/mod/core.html#accessfilename
[11] http://httpd.apache.org/docs/2.2/mod/mpm_common.html#listen
[12] http://httpd.apache.org/docs/2.2/mod/core.html#servername
[13] http://httpd.apache.org/docs/2.2/mod/core.html#options
[14] http://httpd.apache.org/docs/2.2/mod/core.html#allowoverride
[15] http://httpd.apache.org/docs/2.2/mod/core.html#serveralias

Network administration Linux / ProFTPD

FTP is a file sharing protocol.

An FTP server provides some disk directory, and manages authentication password. It connects to the server with an FTP client.

This document presents the configuration of a server ProFTPd [1] under Debian. The management of access rights and configuration are very similar to those of Apache.

Installation and launching

On Debian, ProFTPD is available in a package and can be installed with the command

apt-get install proftpd

It is also possible to configure poour its own needs from source. This specifies the modules to use.

tar zxvf proftpd-1.xxtar.gz
CD proftpd-1.xx
./configure --with-modules=mod_ratio: mod_sql make

make installproftpd

It automatically launches the installation and startup.

The script to start, stop or restart is /etc/init.d/proftpd.

Configuration file

The main configuration file is /etc/proftpd/proftpd.conf.

All the instructions are described on the website of ProFTPD [2]. The main controls are the following :

ServerName " " name ""
description = Indicates the server name that will appear on customers

AccessGrantMsg " " message ""
description = Welcome Message.
comment = The message can contain wildcards such as% u (here the name of the user)

<Limit ...> ... </ Limit>
description = Allows or denies the use of certain FTP commands. comments =

For example the next section authorizes the MKDIR command only users foo and bar:

<Limit MKDIR>
    Allow foo bar
    Deny All
</ Limit>

ServerType " type "
description = Determines how the server receives the
network connections.
comments =
If the type is' standalone ", a parent process will be launched and listen on the network. If the
 type is " inet ", the server will be launched
by inetd (tcp_wrapper).
In all cases there will be a process launched by FTP connection.

MaxInstances 30
description = Limits the number of simultaneous processes allowed

user nobody
Group nobody
description = indicate that the server is to be performed with the group IDs and user nobody

ExtendedLog /var/log/ftp.log
description = specifies the log file name

umask 022
description = specifies the rights to " remove " 'to files created on FTP. 022 means that write
permissions are removed from the group and " others " for any new file.

AllowOverwrite it
description = allows a user to overwrite a file that belongs to him.

UseFtpUsers it
description = active use of the / etc / ftpusers which gives the user list who does " 'not' " access to the FTP server.

AllowUser " list of users "

description = to be placed in a context <Limit ...> ... </ Limit> defines who is authorized to perform the block control " Limit 'current.

DenyUser " list of users "

description = to place in a context <Limit ...> ... </ Limit> defines who is not allowed to execute the control of the current limit block.

AllowStoreRestart
description = allow clients to resume uploads to the server.

DefaultChdir / var / ftp
description = Indicates the default directory of the server.
comment = Users are placed in this directory when logging.

DefaultRoot / var / ftp
description = declares that directory as the file system root.

UserRatio
description = allows management ratios.
comments =
UserRatio " name " 2 10 5 4096 </ code> indicates that the user " name " is entitled to recover two files on the server each time that he will introduce.

It gives it to start a credit of 10 files.
Moreover, to 1 byte filed, it will receive 5 bytes and holds a 4KB credit. Instead of a name can also be used * that defines default ratios.

SaveRatios it

description = used to specify that we want to save the credit of each user between sessions.

RatioFile / ratio / RatioFile

RatioTempFile / ratio / RatioTempFile

description = indicate the file names to store information on users ratios.

FileRatioErrMsg "You do not have enough downloaded files"
ByteRatioErrMsg "You do not have enough of bytes downloaded"
description = indicate that a user has exceeded its quota by messages.

<Directory " " directory> ... </ Directory>

description = This section provides the rights to the directory and everything in it.

comments =

For example :

<Directory / var / ftp / ratio>
    <Limit ALL>
        Deny ALL
    </ Limit>
    HideNoAccess it
</ Directory>

Here, we prohibit any operation on the ratio repertoire thanks to <Limit ALL>.

HideNoAccess
description = Cover all items inaccessible to users.

<Anonymous " directory "> ... </ Anonymous>
description = Configure anonymous access
comments =
example:

<Anonymous / home / ftp>
  # After anonymous login, passes under the user / ftp group. user ftp

  Group ftp

  # Matches the login "anonymous" in unix account "ftp" anonymous ftp UserAlias

  # Allow accounts without "shell" is often the case the account "ftp" RequireValidShell off

  # Prohibits willing everywhere
  <Directory *>
    <Limit WRITE>
     DenyAll
    </ Limit>
  </ Directory>

  # Allows writing in "incoming" but not reading <Directory incoming>
    <Limit READ>
     DenyAll
    </ Limit> <Limit
  STOR>
     AllowAll </
  Limit>
  </ Directory>
</ Anonymous>

For the server to take into account the new configuration file, reload the daemon with:
/etc/init.d/proftpd restart

Example proftpd.conf file:

1. This is a basic ProFTPD configuration file (rename it to # 'proftpd.conf' for
2. actual use. It Establishes a single server
3. It Assumes That You-have a user / group
4. "Nobody" for normal operation.

ServerName "ProFTPd Linux Service" ServerType standalone DefaultServer it

1. To allow clients to summarize the downloads, very useful.
2. Remember to set to off if you-have for an incoming ftp upload.

AllowStoreRestart it

1. Port 21 is the standard FTP

port. Port 45000

1. Umask 022 is a good standard umask to prevent prevention new dirs and files
2. from being white group and world writable.

umask 022

1. Limiting bandwidth read:

RateReadBPS 14000

1. To prevent prevention DoS attacks, set the maximum number of child pro cesses
2. to 30. If you need to allow more than 30 concurrent connections
3. at once, simply Increase this value. That Note this ONLY works
4. In standalone mode, in inetd fashion shoulds you use an inetd server
5. That Allows you to limit maximum number of pro cesses per serving
6. (Such as xinetd)

MaxInstances 30

1. Set the user and group que la Normally server runs at. User

nobody Group nogroup

1. Maximum number of clients
2. MaxClients 3

1. Max Number of Customers per host
2. MaxClientsPerHost 1

1. Maximum number of login attempts

MaxLoginAttempts 3

1. Welcome message after a successful login

AccessGrantMsg "% u Welcome home!"

1. Not to give information on the

server off DeferWelcome

1. Rules limit orders ...

<Limit MKD RNFR RNTO DELE RMD STOR CHMOD CHMOD SITE SITE WRITE XCUP XRMD PWD

XPWD>

DenyAll

</ Limit>
<Global>

DefaultRoot / var / ftp
AllowOverwrite yes
MaxClients 3
MaxClientsPerHost 1
UseFtpUsers it
AllowForeignAddress it
ServerIdent on "ProFTP DUF's Server Ready"
AccessGrantMsg "Welcome to the server% u"

</ Global>

1. Writing for Virtual Server

<VirtualHost ftp.duf.com>

ServerName "My ftp server virtual number 1"
Port 46000
maxclients 3
MaxClientsPerHost 1
DefaultRoot / var / ftp
AccessGrantMsg "Welcome"

</ VirtualHost>

FTP Client

There are many FTP clients. Some are in graphical mode, others in text mode. Internet browsers also allow to connect to an FTP server.

ftp

The simplest and most common customer is the ftp command. It also exists in Windows command line. The available commands are described in the man page. The main ones are: help, open, ls, get, put ...

Navigator

To access an FTP server from a web browser, use a particular address. For anonymous login, you can use ftp: // server / or ftp: // server / path.
To connect with a password, use ftp: // user: password @ server /.

References

[1] http://www.proftpd.org
[2] http://www.proftpd.org/docs/

Network administration Linux / DHCP

The DHCP (for Dynamic Host Configuration Protocol) is a network protocol whose role is to ensure the automatic configuration of network settings of a station, including automatically assigning an IP address and subnet mask.

DHCP is often implemented by stations park administrators as it offers huge advantage to centralize the configuration of stations on a single machine: the DHCP server. The main danger of DHCP is that in case of failure of the DHCP server, no further station accesses the network.

There are two main uses a DHCP server:

- assign a fixed configuration at certain positions (one recognizes them with their MAC address)
- and assign a dynamic configuration to unknown positions.

One can for example give a fixed IP address to some servers, and assign variables addresses to other positions. The protocol is designed for a post which returns to the network gets the same address he had the first time. It is reserved him some time (the lease time).

Configuration

The main configuration file is /etc/dhcp/dhcpd.conf. Its syntax is described in dhcpd.conf man.

It has global options, usually placed at the beginning, and sections for each host or network to be configured.

After each configuration change, you must restart the server:

/etc/init.d/isc-dhcp-server restart

If it does not restart, the detail of the error is usually located in / var / log / syslog

interfaces

By default, the DHCP (Dynamic host configuration protocol) is started on all interfaces. In this case it is imperative to configure a network interface in dhcpd.conf.

To select interfaces on which the server is running, you must edit / etc / default / isc-dhcp-server indicating such

INTERFACES = "eth1 eth2"

It is mandatory to have a section "subnet" (see below) for each network interface.

dynamic Address

To configure a range of addresses to dynamically assign to unknown MAC addresses, subnet section is used in dhcpd.conf. The following example will assign addresses ranging from 192.168.1.101 and 192.168.1.199:

subnet 192.168.1.0 netmask 255.255.255.0 {
    Range 192.168.1.101 192.168.1.199;
}

fixed Address

To give a fixed address for a position, you have to know its MAC address and write a host section. For example the following section assigns the address 192.168.0.47 cobalt station whose MAC address is 00: 13: d4: bd: b7: 9a:

```
host cobalt {
    hardware ethernet 00: 13: d4: bd: b7: 9a;
    fixed-address 192.168.0.47;
}
```

options

The DHCP server can provide other information as the IP address. These options can be set globally by placing them outside any section. They will then apply to all sections that do not redefine. If placed in a special section, they only apply it.

The domain-name-servers option eg to indicate the position addresses of the DNS servers. The option indicates the gateway routers.

All options are described in the man page. One can also consult this internet documentation [1].

References

[1] http://www.linuxmanpages.com/man5/dhcpd.conf.5.php

Network administration Linux / netfilter

Netfilter is a module which filters and manipulate network packets that pass through the system.

It provides Linux :

- functions firewall including machine control who can log on which ports, from outside to inside or from inside to outside the network;
- of address translation (NAT) to share an internet connection (masquerading), hide the LAN machines, or redirect connections;
- and of logging traffic network.

iptables is the order for configuring Netfilter.

Operation

Netfilter intercepts network packets to different parts of the system (at the reception prior to transmit them to process, prior to sending them to the network card, etc.). The intercepted packets pass through channels that will determine what the system should do with the packet. By changing these channels we will be able to block some packets and pass others.

filtering

In its simplest operation, Netfilter lets take or pass the packets in and out.

It provides for that three main channels:

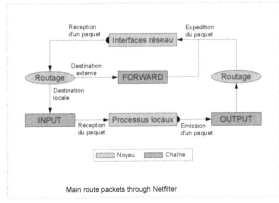

Main route packets through Netfilter

- an INPUT chain to filter packets to the system,
- an OUTPUT chain to filter packets transmitted by the system process,
- and a FORWARD chain for filtering packets that the system must pass.

By adding rules in these chains can be pass or discard packets based on certain criteria.

Chains

A string is a set of rules that indicate what to do packets that pass through.

When a packet arrives in a chain:

- Netfilter watches the first rule in the chain,
- then see if the criteria of the rule corresponds to the packet.
- If the packet matches, the target is executed (discard the packet, pass up, etc.).
- Otherwise, Netfilter takes the new rule and compares the packet. And so on until the last rule.
- If no rules have interrupted the course of the chain, the default policy is applied.

Rules

A rule is a combination of criteria and a target. When all the criteria corresponding to the packet, the packet is sent to the target.

The available criteria and possible actions depend on the manipulated chain.

Syntax

The syntax for iptables and all options are described in the man page.

For each setting there is typically a long form with two hyphens (eg --append) and a short form with a single hyphen (eg -A). Use one or the other does not matter, they are equivalent. Both possibilities are often represented in the documentation in the form --append | -A.

The parameters shown in brackets (eg [-t <table>]) are optional.

Which is located between upper and lower (e.g. <table>) must be replaced by a value.

The general form for use iptables is the following:

iptables [-t <table>] <command> <options>

The default table is the filter table.

Orders

The main controls are:

--list | -L [<string>]

Displays the rules in channels or just the selected channel.

If the -v parameter is placed before this command, the number of packets passed through each rule will also be displayed.

--append | -A <string> <criteria> j <target>

Adds a rule at the end of the <string> string. If all the criteria match the packet, it is sent to the target. See below for a description of the criteria and possible target.

--insert | -I <string> <criteria> j <target> As --append but

adds the rule to the beginning of the string. --delete | -D

<string> <criteria> j <target>

Deletes the corresponding rule in the chain.

--flush | -F [<string>]

Clear all rules from chain. If no string is specified, all chains will be flushed from the table.

--policy | -P <string> <target>

Determines the target when no rules interrupted the course and that the packet reaches the end of string.

criteria

Possible criteria are numerous. Here are a few :

--protocol | -p <protocol> [!]

The protocol <protocol>. Possible protocols are TCP, UDP, ICMP, all, or a numeric value. The values of / etc / protocols are also usable. If an exclamation point is before the Protocol, the criterion will correspond to package only if it is not specified protocol.

--source | [!] -s <address> [/ <mask>]

The source address is <address>. If a mask is specified, only active parts of the mask will be compared. By example when writing -s   192.168.5.0/255.255.255.0, all addresses between 192.168.5.0 and 192.168.5.255 match. We can also write the mask in the form of a number of bits (/ 8 corresponds to 255.0.0.0, / 24 to 255.255.255.0, etc.) The default mask is / 32 (/255.255.255.255) or the entire address.

An exclamation point will not match the package if it is not the source address.

--destination | [!] -d <address> [/ <mask>]

As --source but for the destination address.

--dport [!] <port>

The destination port <port>. It is mandatory to specify the protocol (-p tcp or udp -p), as in other protocols no port concept.

--sport [!] <port>

As --dport but the source port.

-i <interface>

The network interface where the packet originated. Usable only in the INPUT chain.

-o <interface>

The network interface that goes from the package. Usable only in the OUTPUT and FORWARD chains.

--icmp-<type>

If the protocol is icmp, specifies a specific type. Examples of types: echo-request for sending a "Ping" echo-reply to the answer to "ping"

targets

The main targets are:

j ACCEPT

Allows the packet to go and interrupts his journey in the chain.

j DROP

Throw the package without notifying the sender. The path of the chain is interrupted.

j REJECT

As DROP but prevents the transmitter that the packet is discarded. The response sent to the transmitter is also a package that will satisfy the exit rules to pass.

-j LOG [--log-level <level>] [--log-prefix <prefix>]

Save the package in the system logs. In <level> by default, the package is displayed on the main console system.
This target is useful to see some packages that pass (for debugging or to alert).

single use

The principle is quite simple to understand. An IP packet arrives at your machine, you must choose what you do. You can accept (ACCEPT), reject (REJECT) or denier (DROP). The difference between the last two modes, is to prevent or not the sender that his package has been refused (with REJECT is prevented, but not with DROP).

Three types of packages can pass through the firewall. Outgoing packets (OUTPUT), inbound (INPUT) or "passing", that is to say that only bounce on the router must redirect FORWARD).

To organize the rules of acceptance / rejection, the procedure is as follows: - INPUT, OUTPUT, FORWARD, are called channels - rule is a set of attributes that corresponds (or not) a package: source IP, IP destination, source port, destination port, protocol. . . - when a packet passes through the firewall, it is routed to the corresponding string - then the rules of the chain are tested one by one in order, on the package. When the packet matches a rule, it stops. If the rule says ACCEPT, the packet is accepted. If it says DROP, it is ignored. If REJECT states, it is rejected with acquittal. The following rules are not tested.

- if no rule matches the packet, the default policy is applied. It may be set to ACCEPT, DROP or REJECT. It is safer (but longer to implement) use a DROP default policy and create rules ACCEPT.
The iptables syntax is:

iptables | I string -i (or -o) -p protocol interface --sport [startingPort [:
port_fin] [, autre_port ...]] --dport [startingPort [: port_fin] [, autre_port]]
-s -d adresse_source adresse_dest policy j

There are of course many other options.

Create and apply rules

All iptables commands are typed directly on the Terminal command line. It is more practical to include them in a script file and make the script executable (chmod + x). Give only the minimum rights to that file so it can not be read and modified by everyone. File Example:

#! / Bin / sh
 # Clear all the rules first of all, to from a **based**

 # own and know exactly what you are doing
iptables -F

 # Set a default policy is the most normal of all **prohibit by**

 # default and allow only certain packets.
 # "DROP" drops packets, "REJECT" rejects with acquittal **the sender**

 # often puts "DROP" to the INPUT (we do not give information
a
 # possible pirate) and "REJECT" for the OUTPUT and FORWARD (one can **so**

 # retrieve information about itself) but does not allow iptables REJECT

```
#  the default policy iptables -P INPUT
DROP iptables -P OUTPUT DROP
iptables -P FORWARD DROP


#  Allow traffic on the loopback interface: -A INPUT -i lo iptables
j ACCEPT
iptables OUTPUT -o lo -j ACCEPT


#  Then it's up to you to add the rules to make function


#  the services you want to use on your machine.
```

Some examples

To empty the INPUT chain of the filter table (the default table):

    INPUT iptables --flush

The default policy is to accept all packets, which is usually a poor choice for safety.

To change this rule to the FORWARD chain of the filter table:

    iptables -P FORWARD DROP

To pass the packets on Harbor *telnet* coming from a LAN (Long form):

    INPUT iptables --append --protocol --destination tcp port telnet --source 192.168.13.0/24 --jump
    ACCEPT

To ignore the other incoming packets on Port (software) | harbor *telnet* (Short form):

    -A INPUT -p tcp iptables --dport telnet j DROP

To reject incoming packets on the Harbor 3128, often used by *proxies* :

    -A INPUT -p tcp iptables --dport 3128 -j REJECT To allow telnet

to your machine (telnet server):

    -A INPUT -p tcp iptables --dport telnet j ACCEPT iptables -A
    OUTPUT -p tcp telnet --sport j ACCEPT

To allow telnet from your machine (telnet client):

    iptables OUTPUT p tcp telnet --dport j ACCEPT iptables -A INPUT -
    p tcp telnet --sport j ACCEPT

Destination NAT:

iptables -t nat -A PREROUTING -p tcp --dport 80 -j DNAT --to 192.168.0.1

The FTP case

FTP is difficult to manage with a firewall because it uses multiple connections. When connecting via FTP to a server, we created a so-called control connection for sending commands to the server. Then for each file transfer and each directory listing, a new data connection is created.

The firewall can very well handle the control connection, but not those for transfer as they are made of indeterminate ports. On some FTP servers can be set a range of ports to use, and in this case can be simple NAT.

It is also possible to use the "conntrack ftp". It is a module that inspects Netfilter FTP connections control to detect data connections. He then tells the kernel that these connections are linked to another connection (RELATED). To enable these connections with iptables using the state module.

This requires ip_conntrack_ftp load module

modprobe ip_conntrack_ftp

And authorize RELATED connections for input and output:

iptables INPUT -m state --state RELATED -j ACCEPT iptables -A
OUTPUT -m state --state RELATED -j ACCEPT

Network administration Linux / TCP Wrapper

The super inetd service to control and restrict access to certain network services. These are managed by inetd and are no longer in a mode "standalone".

Inetd uses tcpd daemon that intercepts connection requests to a service and check through the hosts.allow and hosts.deny if the client is allowed to use this service. On current versions of Linux, it is installed by default. By cons it is not active in his party access control.

Inetd is an element to implement to secure a machine running Linux, it may not, however, completely replace a real firewall.

The principle

When you want to connect to a remote machine with telnet for example, inetd intercepts your connection request and checks in inetd.conf if the telnet service is usable. If the answer is positive, your application is passed to tcpd that checks in hosts.allow and hosts.deny if you have the right to log on telnet, if this is the case your connection request will be allowed, otherwise you will rejected. In all cases and this is another function tcp_wrappers, tcpd forward to syslog (log daemon) your request (this request will be in the log, / var / log / security).

The installation

By default it is installed with most distributions, but if the package is installed:

tcp_wrappers-x ..... rpm. Tcp_wrappers uses the following files: tcpd, inetd, inetd.conf, hosts.allow, hosts.deny, tcpdchk, tcpdmatch.

Configuration: inetd.conf

This file is located in / etc. You can enable or disable services here, placing a # in front of the line or removing it, and then forcing the reading of the file with the command killall -HUP inetd. It is possible to add other services in this file.

Here is one commented:

```
#  Version: \ @ (#) / etc / inetd.conf
#  The first lines are used by inetd
#
#echo stream tcp nowait root internal
#echo        dgram       udp        wait      internal root
#discard        stream       tcp        nowait       internal root
#discard        dgram       udp        wait      internal root
#daytime        stream       tcp        nowait       internal root
#daytime        dgram       udp        wait      root      internal
#chargen        stream       tcp        nowait       root      internal
#chargen        dgram       udp        wait      root      internal
#time      stream       tcp        nowait       root      internal
#time      dgram       udp        wait      root      internal
#
#ftp and telnet are two widely used services.
#lls are not especially secure. telnet can be remplacépar SSH is much more secure.
#
# ftp        stream       tcp nowait        root        / Usr / sbin / tcpd
in.ftpd telnet        stream tcp        nowait        root        / Usr / sbin / tcpd
in.telnetd
#
#Shell, login,        exec and talk are comsat        BSD protocols.
#Essayez not        not use them.
#lls contains holes at                            Security.
# shell        stream tcp nowait        root / usr / sbin / tcpd
in.rshd login stream tcp nowait root / usr / sbin / tcpd in.rlogind
#exec stream        tcp nowait        root / usr / sbin / tcpd in.rexecd
#comsat dgram udp wait        root / usr / sbin / tcpd in.comsat
udp talk gram        nobody.tty wait / usr / sbin / tcpd in.talkd
ntalk dgram        udp wait        nobody.tty / usr / sbin / tcpd in.ntalkd
#dtalk stream tcp wait nobody.tty / usr / sbin / tcpd in.dtalkd #

#  POP3 and IMAP are mail servers.
#  To activate only if you use them.
#  forget pop2
# 2 pop-stream        tcp nowait root
```

/ Usr / sbin / tcpd ipop2d

Pop-3 stream   tcp nowait root

/ Usr / sbin / tcpd   ipop3d

#imap stream   tcp nowait root

/ Usr / sbin / tcpd   imapd

#

#The UUCP service is a way to send files between machines.

#The service is practically no longer used.

#Evitez use.

#uucp stream   tcp   nowait   uucp

/ Usr / sbin / tcpd / usr / lib / uucp / uucico -l

#ftp and bootp are used to allow machines

  Clients who do not have

boot disk, receive an IP address to load the system. #TFTP do not have authentication system it

#est a huge security hole. # You must absolutely avoid using

tftpdgram udpwaitroot

/ Usr / sbin / tcpd in.tftpd

Bootps dgram udp wait root / usr / sbin / tcpd bootpd #Finger, cfinger, systat and netstat are not

dangerous in themselves, but they

provide information on accounts and #utilisateurs your system.

#He so do not use them.

finger stream tcp nowait nobody / usr / sbin / tcpd in.fingerd #cfinger stream

tcp nowait root / usr / sbin / tcpd in.cfingerd #systat stream tcp nowait guest /

usr / sbin / tcpd / bin / ps -auwwx

#netstat stream tcp nowait guest / usr / sbin / tcpd   / Bin / netstat -f inet

Auth Authentication Service provides information about the user auth stream tcp wait root

/usr/sbin/in.identd in.identd -e -o

end of inetd.conf linuxconf stream tcp wait root / bin / linuxconf linuxconf --http

The # in front of a line makes the idle line, so the service unavailable. If you do not use a service, visit the inactive.

Here is a description of some options. Consider the following line:

ftp stream tcp nowait root / usr / sbin / tcpd in.ftpd

- **ftp:** service name, as declared in / etc / services
- **stream:** type of data transport service (there are stream tcp, udp for dgram, raw for IP)
- **tcp:** protocol name as it exists in / etc / protocols
- **wait:** standby state, if the state is wait inetd must wait until the server has returned the socket before resuming listening. Is used rather wait with dgram types and raw. Alternatively nowait which allows to dynamically allocate sockets for use with the stream types.
- **root:** User name under which the daemon turns

• **/ Usr / sbin / tcpd in.ftpd** Path to in.ftpd program launched by inetd (it is possible here to add the program's startup options.

Hosts.allow and hosts.deny

You will find these files in the / etc directory.

The first file is read hosts.allow and hosts.deny. If a request is allowed in hosts.allow file while it is accepted, whatever the content of hosts.deny. If a request does not meet any rule, whether in hosts.allow or hosts.deny then it is allowed. In a word if you do not put anything in hosts.deny, then you have nothing. Here is a small example in simple cases is sufficient:

hosts.allow

```
#  hosts.allow
ALL: LOCAL
in.ftpd: 192.168.0, 10.194.168.0 / 255.255.255.0, 192.168.1.1.
in.telnetd: .iut.u-clermont1.fr
```

It allows all the ports for local access, and we allow ftp to machines from the 192.168.0.0 network and the machines of 10.194.168.0 network with another notation and finally the only machine that has the address 192.168.1.1

hosts.deny

```
# hosts.deny
ALL: ALL
```

Hosts.deny is simple to understand, it prohibits any default. Hosts.allow indicates the services that I want to allow (The service name must match the name that is in inetd.conf). the syntax is:

daemon [, daemon ...] customer [, customer ...] [: option: option ...]

This syntax is the same in both files hosts.allow and hosts.deny.

Utilities tcp wrappers

• tcpdchk -av: displays the configuration tcp wrappers
• tcpdmatch in.ftpd localhost to simulate a connection on in.ftpd

see xinetd equivalent of tcp_wrappers, but with more options.

Network administration Linux / Tcpdump

In an ethernet hub connected by a network (or hub), each machine receives all packets traveling on the network. In normal operation, the NIC shall approve only the packets intended for them, but we can make sure they pass all the packets to the system.

Hubs are used less and less. They are usually replaced by switches (or switch) who can determine (based on MAC addresses) on which cable you need to send a package. The machines therefore generally receive the packages intended for them.

The tcpdump utility to inspect the packets that are received and transmitted by a network card.

filtering

You can select packages to "listen" on the basis of expressions. So will not be displayed / processed the information for which the result of the expression is checked. An expression consists of primitives and logical operators.

A primitive is an identifier preceded by key words that indicate the type of the identifier. For example the original src port 21 contains the following elements:

- src keyword that indicates that the identifier covers only the packet source
- the keyword port which indicates that the identifier is the port package
- the identifier 21

The primitive corresponds to the source port 21.

Similarly, the primitive src ether 00: 11: 22: 33: 44: 55 indicates the ethernet address (or MAC) source 00: 11: 22: 33: 44: 55.

The most common primitives are:

src <address>

> the source address is <address>

dst <address>

> the destination address is <address>

host <address>

> the source address or destination is <address>

port <port>

> the source port or destination is <port>

src port <port>

> Source port <port>

dst port <port>

> the destination port <port>

portrange <port1> - <port2>

> the port is between <port1> and <port2>. We can identify the origin with key words src or dst and
> protocol with the keywords tcp or udp.

The primitives can be linked with logical operators and, or and not. For example the following expression will find all the packets from tiny but the port is not the ssh port:

src tiny and not ssh port

It is also possible to specify a protocol: udp, tcp, icmp.

options

Several options to modify the behavior of tcpdump:

-i <interface>

> selects the network interface on which tcpdump listening. By default it takes the first active (except lo).

-x

> also displays the data found in the packets, in hexadecimal

-X

> displays data packages in ASCII format

-s <number>

> by default, only the first 68 bytes of data are displayed. This parameter can change this number.

-w

> to specify the path of a file where to save the dump.

Examples

tcpdump src 192.168.0.1

Here, the only listed packages are those from 192.168.0.1. We can also state our preferences by adding a criterion:

tcpdump src 192.168.0.1 and port 80

There, the only port of interest is 80 (http).

Here is a complete line that really lets the packets from 192.168.0.1 to 212.208.225.1, port 53 UDP.

tcpdump -X -s -x 0 src and dst 192.168.0.1 212.208.225.1 and port 53 and udp

We asked the packet content display in hexadecimal and ASCII formats (-x -X) and that, whatever their size (-s 0). We get the desired information:

```
0x0000:     4500  003b  0000  4000  4011 CA00 c1fd d9b4      E ..; .. @ @ ........
0x0010:     c1fc 1303  80A1  0035  0027 213d  14C2   0100  ....... 5. '! = ....
0x0020:     0001  0000  0000  0000  0377 7777  056C   696th  ......... www.lin
0x0030:     7578  036f  7267  0000  0100 01              ux.org .....
```

Network administration Linux / SSH

SSH stands for secure shell. This is a protocol that allows for secure connections (ie encrypted) between a server and an SSH client.

It can be used to connect to a remote machine as telnet, to transfer files securely or to create tunnels. The tunnels enable secure protocols that are not passing the data through an SSH connection.

The SSH key system

asymmetric cryptography

SSH uses asymmetric cryptography RSA or DSA. In asymmetric cryptography, each person has a key pair: a public key and a private key. The public key can be published freely while everyone must keep his secret private key. Knowing the public key does not allow to deduce the private key.

If person A wants to send a confidential message to person B, A encrypts the message with the public key of B and sends to B on a channel that is not necessarily secure. Only B can decrypt the message using its private key.

symmetric cryptography

SSH also uses symmetric cryptography. The principle is simple: if A wants to send a confidential message to B, A and B must first have the same secret key A encrypts the message with the secret key and sends it to B on a channel that is not necessarily secure. B decrypts the message with the secret key.

Any other person in possession of the secret key can decrypt the message.

Symmetric cryptography is much less processor-intensive resources that asymmetric cryptography, but the big problem is the exchange of the secret key between A and B. In the SSL protocol, which is used by Web browsers and SSH, the crypto asymmetric is used at the beginning of communication so that a and B can exchange a secret key in a secure manner, and then subsequently the communication is secured by symmetric cryptography using the exchanged secret key.

SSH Server Configuration

To manipulate the daemon (start, stop, reload the configuration ...), use the command

/etc/init.d/ssh

The SSH server configuration file is / etc / ssh / sshd_config. Not to be confused with / etc / ssh / ssh_config is the SSH client configuration file.

Among the many options, it can be noted:

- **Port 22:** Means that the SSH server listening on port 22, which is the normal SSH port. It is possible to do listen to another port by changing this line.
- **Protocol 2:** Means that the SSH server supports only version 2 of the SSH protocol. It is a version more secure than the protocol version 1. To accept the two protocols, change the line: Protocol 2.1
- **PermitRootLogin No:** Means you can not log in as root via SSH. To log in as root, simply log in normal user and use the su command.
- **X11Forwarding yes:** Authorizes the transfer SSH graphical display.
- **LoginGraceTime 600:** Maximum Connection Time

- **RSAAuthentication yes:** Authentication method.
- **AuthorizedKeysFile .ssh / authorized_keys** file used for 'auto login'
- **PermitEmptyPasswords No:** allows or not the empty password

If the server configuration file has been changed, indicate the sshd daemon to reread its configuration file, with the /etc/init.d/ssh restart command.

If logguer SSH

Two types of authentication are possible: by password and key. In both cases we use the following commands:

ssh -l <login> <address of the SSH server>
ssh <login> @ <address of the SSH server>

password authentication

This is the simplest method. When connecting, the ssh client request the account password. In this case, SSH encrypts the password which prevents to see circulate in clear on the network.

Key Authentication

Instead of authenticating with a password, users can authenticate through asymmetric cryptography and torque of public / private key, as does the SSH server to the SSH client. The public key is placed on the server in the home of the account on which you want to connect. The private key remains on the client. In this case, no password is circulating on the network.

Generate Key

To generate a key pair, use the command:

ssh-keygen -t dsa

Two keys will be generated, a public key (default ~ / .ssh / id_dsa.pub) and a private key (default ~ / .ssh / id_dsa). This is the public key that will be copied to the server.

The generated keys have a default length of 1024 bits, which is now considered sufficient for good protection.

The command asks for a file name to save the private key and a file name to save the public key. By default, the private key is stored in the file $ HOME / .ssh / id_dsa.

The private key is saved with permissions 600. The public key has the same file name followed by ".pub" with permissions 644.

When creating the key, the utility asks for a pass phrase that is a password to protect the private key (2nd protection). The pass phrase is used to encrypt the private key. The pass phrase will be requested every time the private key, that is, every time you log in using this authentication method. A mechanism called ssh-agent allows not to enter the password each time (see the docs).

It is possible to change the pass phrase which protects the private key with the ssh-keygen -p command.

Allow the public key

To allow a key to log on to an account, place $ HOME / .ssh / its public part in the file if you want to authorized_keys of the account in question, on the SSH server. sasa server connect to
on the account, the file is /home/sasa/.ssh/authorized_keys.

To transfer the public key, you can use ftp, scp (file copy via ssh), or a simple copy / paste between two terminals (it's just a long line of ASCII characters).

Each line of authorized_keys corresponds to a public key file allowed to connect. Check that each key is one line, otherwise it does not work.

The $ HOME / .ssh 'should be write-protected, with permissions 755 (or 705). Similarly, the authorized_keys file should not be readable by all (600 for example).

Then, to log, simply proceed as above.

If the private key was recorded in another file $ HOME / .ssh / id_dsa must specify the ssh client:

ssh -i <name of the file containing the private key> <login> @ <server>

SSH agent

An SSH agent is a program that keeps track of private keys. The principle is:

• an agent is launched
• we add key (if the key is encrypted, it is decrypted with the passphrase before being added)
• each ssh, the key of the agent are used in priority

The main advantages are:

• the passphrase is requested only once when it is added to the agent,
• and the agent is able to follow the key on multiple connections.

To start an agent is generally used a command that looks like:

ssh-agent / bin / bash

The SSH agent starting a new shell ("/ bin / bash") in which it will be active. It will be usable only from this shell and the programs to be launched there.

To add a key is used

ssh-add [<file>]

If it does not specify a file, it will use the default key ("~ / .ssh / id_dsa" for SSH 2).

If the key is encrypted, the passphrase will be requested and the decrypted key will be added to the agent.

All SSH connections (with ssh, scp ...) launched from this shell will use the agent and therefore require more passphrase.

Create a "tunnel" encrypted between two stations

SSH is also able to provide encryption to other services (eg FTP) via the port forwarding.

(-L and -R options in the ssh command), as follows:

Consider two stations HOST1 and HOST2. Suppose the HOST1 machine you use the command:

ssh -L p1: HOST2 p2 HOST2

or HOST2:

ssh -R p1: HOST2 p2 HOST1

then you get a secure tunnel through which you can pass any connection, which will be automatically encrypted.

On HOST1 ssh -L p1: HOST2 p2 HOST2 means that when connecting to the port p1, the packets are transmitted to the port p2 of the machine via HOST2 HOST2.

Network administration Linux / Routing

IP and MAC Addresses

Each interface of each computer will be identified by

* IP address: IP address (version 4, IP V 4) identifies a host and a subnet.
  The IP address is coded over 4 bytes - 32 bits. (IP V 6 or IP next generation will be coded on 16 bytes - 128 bits).
* The mac address of its network card (Ethernet card or wireless card) of 6 bytes - 48 bits;

An IP address identifies a host. A gateway is a computer that has multiple interfaces and transmits the packets from one interface to another. The gateway can communicate and different networks. Each network card has a unique MAC address guaranteed by the manufacturer. When a computer has multiple interfaces, each with its own MAC address and IP address. We can see its network configuration ifconfig:

```
$ Ifconfig eth0
eth0           Link encap: Ethernet HWaddr 00: B2: 3A: 24: F3: C4
               inet addr: 192.168.0.2 Bcast: 192.168.0.255 Mask: 255.255.255.0
               inet6 addr: fe80 :: 2C0: 9FFF: fef9: 95b0 / 64 Scope: Link
               UP BROADCAST RUNNING MULTICAST MTU: 1500 Metric: 1
               RX packets: 6 errors: 0 dropped: 0 overruns: 0 frame: 0
               TX packets: 16 errors: 0 dropped: 0 overruns: 0 carrier: 5
               collisions: 0 txqueuelen: 1000
               RX bytes: 1520 (1.4 KiB) TX bytes: 2024 (1.9 KiB)
               Interrupt: 10
```

We see the MAC address 00: B2: 3A: 24: F3: C4 and the IP address 192.168.0.2. This means that the first byte of the IP address is equal to 192, the second 168, the third byte is zero, and the fourth is 2.

Subnets

Classes subnets

Until the 1990s, IPv4 addresses were organized into subnets. Each subnet has an address, which is part of the IP address of the machine that subnet.

For example, the IP address 192.168.4.35 belongs to the subnet 192.168.4, sometimes also noted 192.168.4.0.

Subnets are organized into classes. Each class subnet corresponds to networks that may contain a number of machines.

- Class A: addresses of 1.0.0.0 to 127.0.0.0. The network identifier is then 8 bits and machine IDs are 24 bits (several million units per subnet;
- Class B: 128.0.0.0 of addresses to 191.255.0.0. The network identifier is then 16 bits and machine identifiers are 16-bit (more than 65 000 machines per subnet);
- Class C: addresses from 192.0.0.0 to 223.255.255.0. The network identifier is then 24 bits and machine IDs are 8 bits (at most 254 machines per subnet, numbered 1 to 254);

Subnet mask

A subnet mask is a given on 4 bytes, with the address of the subnet, characterizes the subnet IP.

A bit of the subnet mask is 1 if for all the IP addresses of the subnet, the same bit is the same for the IP address and subnet.

For example, for the Class A network 37.0.0.0 with the mask of 255.0.0.0 subnet, the first 8 bits of all the subnet IP addresses are worth 37.

Another example for the subnet Class C 193.56.49.0 and mask 255.255.255.0 subnet, the first 24 bits of all the subnet IP is 193.56.49.

It may appoint a sub-network address and mask, but you can also designate the subnet giving only the number of bits of the mask. This is called, to use the two examples above, the 37.0.0.0/8 subnet or 193.56.49.0/24 subnet.

routing

Routing enables communication across subnets. A gateway (gateway in English) is in communication with different subnets on different interfaces and provides communication between different subnets (see Figure 8.1).

routes

A road set on a station is a path to be taken by packets to a certain subnet. For example (see Figure 8.1) a station called station 1 of 112.65.77.8 IP address on a network 112.0.0.0/8.

(Fig 8.1. EXAMPLE gateway communicating two networks)

It is connected to a gateway that has the IP 112.65.123.3 in this network on its eth0. The gateway is also connected to the 192.168.0.0/24 network through its eth1 interface that has IP 192.168.0.1. If the station 1 wants to communicate directly with the station called station 6 of 192.168.0.2 IP address on the 192.168.0.0/24 network, three conditions must be met;

- A road must be defined on the station 1 indicating that the packets destined for the 192.168.0.0/24 network must pass through the gateway 112.65.123.3. For this, you can use the route command:

route add -net 192.168.0.0/24 gw 112.65.123.3

* A road must be defined on the station 6 indicating that the packets to the 112.0.0.0/8 network must pass

   through the gateway 192.168.0.1; For this, you can use the route command:

route add -net 192.168.0.1 gw 112.0.0.0/8

* The gateway must be configured to transmit (or forwarder) IP packets from one network to another, which is

   done by one of the following commands (both are the same, no need to repeat):

echo 1> / proc / sys / net / ipv4 / ip_forward
sysctl -w net.ipv4.ip_forward = 1

Note: You must repeat these commands after a reboot. To avoid revive these commands manually, you can put them in the boot scripts start with the update-rc.d (debian)). To add a script to my_ initialization script:

mv my_script /etc/init.d
update-rc.d defaults my_script

If the IP-forwarding is activated via one sysctl, the standard file this parameter configuration is /etc/sysctl.conf, where the line is already comment.

You can see the state of the roads with the command route -n. For example, station 1:

route -n

Destination	Gateway	Genmask	Flags	Metric Ref		use Iface
192.168.0.0	112.65.123.3	255.255.255.0	U	0	0	0 eth2
etc ...						

On the station 6

route -n

Destination	Gateway	Genmask	Flags	Metric Ref		use Iface
112.0.0.0	192.168.0.1	255.0.0.0	U	0	0	0 wlan0
etc ...						

To delete a route, for instance to 193.86.46.0/24 196.24.52.1 network via a gateway, it is:

route del -net 193.86.46.0/24 gw 196.24.52.1

Default route (gateway)

When we defined a number of routes on a station, you can define a special route for IP packets à destination for which no other road networks. We call such a route a default route. In general, this is the road that must be used to go online. We use the 0.0.0.0 network (255.255.255.255 mask). To set a default route is little used road. For example, to set the default route via the gateway 194.56.87.1:

route add default gw 194.56.87.1

To remove this road:

route del default gw 194.56.87.1

NAT and masquerading

When a host with an IP address on a local network tries to connect to a larger network, for example on the Internet, via a gateway, the host needs an IP address on the vast network. For this, either the LAN addresses are asked that are routed on the global network, but it must then apply to reserve a range of addresses on the global network, is the administrator of the gateway has the ability to pay IP gateway to local network machines. For this, iptables is used with NAT. For example, if the gateway connects to the internet via its eth0, just run the following command on the bridge:

iptables -t nat -A POSTROUTING -o eth0 -j MASQUERADE

Every machine on the local network (eg 192.168.0.0/24) that connects to the internet via this gateway will then have the IP address of the gateway on the Internet. It can also give the LAN machines another IP address that you specify with -to:

iptables -t nat -A POSTROUTING -o eth0 -j SNAT --to 193.56.17.9

We will have a more complete overview of the opportunities iptables in the literature Netfilter.

redirection

It is also possible to change the destination of a packet. This is useful when you want to hide a machine behind another: the client connects to a server that will forward all packets to another. For the customer it is transparent, it is as if it was the first server that replied. This is called the Destination NAT (DNAT). Fxample to redirect all port 22 connections to the server 192.168.1.12:

iptables -t nat -A PREROUTING -p tcp --dport 22 -j DNAT --to 192.168.1.12

www.ingramcontent.com/pod-product-compliance
Lightning Source LLC
Chambersburg PA
CBHW070901070326
40690CB00009B/1949